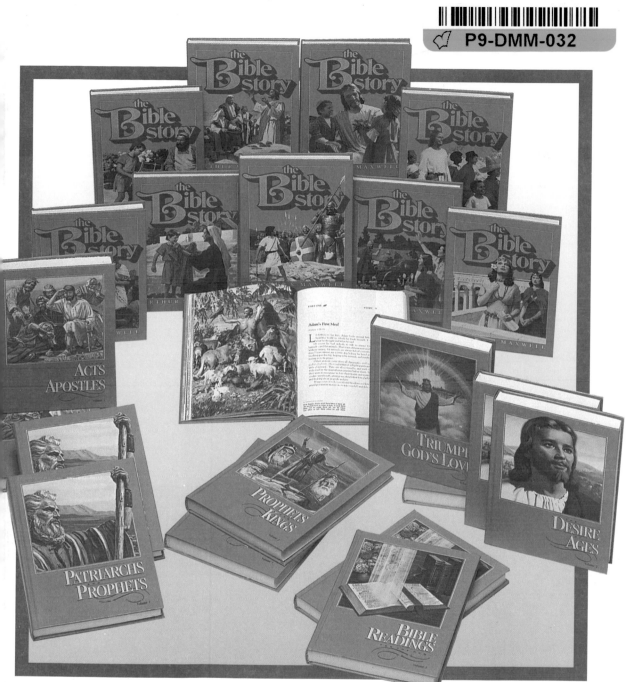

The Bible Reference Library

The Bible Reference Library is *The Bible Story* for adults. Find out what Bible stories tell you about God and how He relates to people today. Get answers to tough questions such as "If God is love, why does He allow suffering?" If you want to know exactly what the Bible can tell you about the past, present, and future, you'll treasure this 12 volume set.

**For information
on how to obtain these beatiful books for your home, mail the postage-paid card today.**

A Lifetime Treasure

Lovingly Presented

_____

_____

_____

the Bible Story

The Book of Beginnings ❖ Volume One

Arthur S. Maxwell
Author of Uncle Arthur's *Bedtime Stories*

When Arthur S. Maxwell wrote *The Bible Story,* he used the King James Version of the Bible, closely following its narrative. This edition continues that tradition and draws from other translations using language that today's children readily understand.

NEWLY REVISED AND ILLUSTRATED
More than 400 stories in 10 Volumes Covering the Entire Bible From Genesis to Revelation

REVIEW AND HERALD® PUBLISHING ASSOCIATION
HAGERSTOWN, MD 21740
www.thebiblestory.com

All illustrations are by
Herbert Rudeen except those
individually credited.

Unless otherwise noted, all
Bible verses are from the *Holy
Bible, New International Version*.
Copyright © 1973, 1978, 1983,
International Bible Society.
Used by permission of
Zondervan Bible Publishers.
Scriptures credited to ICB are
quoted from the *International
Children's Bible, New Century
Version,* copyright © 1983,
1986, 1988 by Word
Publishing, Dallas, Texas
75039. Used by permission.
Bible texts credited to TEV are
from the *Good News Bible*—
Old Testament: Copyright ©
American Bible Society 1976;
New Testament: Copyright ©
American Bible Society 1966,
1971, 1976. Bible texts credited
to NRSV are from the New
Revised Standard Version
Bible, copyright © 1989,
Division of Christian
Education of the National
Council of Churches of Christ
in the U.S.A.

This book was
Revised by Cheryl Holloway
Edited by Richard W. Coffen
Cover art by Harry Anderson

PRINTED IN U.S.A.

R&H Cataloging Service
Maxwell, Arthur Stanley,
1896-1970
    The Bible story.
    1. Bible stories.   I. Title.
II. Holloway, Cheryl Woolsey,
1956-
        220.9505

ISBN 0-8280-0795-0

**What fun it is to blow
on the dandelion seed
balls and see the soft
furry particles fly away
into the air. This is how
the wind scatters the
seeds of trees and of
plants everywhere.**

PAINTING BY RUSSELL HARLAN

A Word From the Author

THE BIBLE is the most wonderful storybook ever written. It is full of stories, all the way from the first chapter of Genesis to the last chapter of Revelation.

These stories have been told over and over again for thousands of years, yet they are new and fresh and fascinating to every generation. They need to be retold today, so that the boys and girls of the late twentieth and early twenty-first centuries may see their beauty and catch their inspiration.

It is one of the strangest paradoxes of our time that just when the Bible is enjoying its widest circulation, millions of copies being sold every year, fewer people than ever seem to be reading it. Because in countless homes family worship and the reading of the Bible have been neglected, and parents themselves seldom open its pages, a whole generation is growing up with little or no knowledge of this wonderful Book.

Most modern children have heard little or nothing about the great Bible characters of ancient times, so familiar to their grandparents. Their heroes are not Daniel, Paul, and Peter, but fictionalized heroes whose conduct does not always lend support to traditional values. They have never heard of the love of Jesus, and thus have been robbed of the greatest treasure their minds and hearts could possess. No wonder there is so much juvenile delinquency, youthful vandalism, and lawlessness.

In the author's opinion no greater contribution could be made to the welfare of society and the peace of the world than to lead children to love the Bible—to enjoy its stories, appreciate its teachings, adopt its standards, and find its God.

In writing *The Bible Story* the author has tried not only to tell the dear old stories in language that the boys and girls of today can understand but also to reveal the gold thread that binds these stories together—the love of God for the children of the human race, and His wondrous plan for their redemption.

The overall purpose has been to provide what might be called a Bible for children by retelling all the old familiar stories in language that modern boys and girls can both understand and enjoy.

All these retold stories are original. No paragraph or sentence has been borrowed from the work of any other author. In this sense, it is an altogether new work, adapted to the needs and desires of today's children.

Although an endeavor has been made to use simple words that the youngest child who is able to read can easily understand, these volumes are not intended to be readers for preschool children. It is presumed that parents of these little ones will read the stories to them, explaining the longer words as may be necessary.

The Bible Story provides the widest coverage of any Bible storybook on the market. In its pages will be found all the stories suitable for telling to children, from Genesis to Revelation. In the telling of these stories the Bible narrative has been carefully adhered to without any addition of fanciful speculations.

Gladly the author confesses that in pursuing this undertaking he has caught a fresh glimpse of the wonder and glory of the Book of books. Over and over again, in retelling the story of Creation and the Flood, the lives of patriarchs and prophets, the life and ministry of Jesus Christ, or the witness and martyrdom of the founders of the early church, he has seemed to hear, echoing down the centuries, those inexpressibly beautiful words "God so loved the world."

Gratitude is due to the publishers, who with rare vision and enterprise have arranged for the illustration of these volumes with original paintings by some of the finest artists of our day.

It is the hope and prayer of the author that, as a result of the publication of *The Bible Story*, thousands of children all around the world will be led to find new joy and interest in the Bible, and accept it for themselves, as indeed it is, the Word of the living God.

PAINTING BY HARRY ANDERSON

Although Adam and Eve had been banished from Eden, they were blessed with children and given a beautiful home in which they laughed and sang and worshiped the Creator.

To boys and girls in
every land and to all
who love the Bible

DEDICATION

PAINTING BY RUSSELL HARLAN

C O N T E N T S

PART ONE—Stories of Creation

PART TWO—Stories of Eden and the Fall

PART THREE—Stories About Noah and the Flood

PART FOUR—Stories About Abraham, Isaac, and Lot

PART ONE

Stories of

Creation

(Genesis 1:1-2:7)

Back to the Beginning

(Genesis 1:1)

HAVE you ever wondered how everything in the world began? I suppose so. Most boys and girls do at some time or other.

Those beautiful flowers in your garden, for instance— sweet peas, snapdragons, hollyhocks, pansies, asters—where did they come from?

"Seeds," you say.

True, but where did the seeds come from?

From other flowers, of course, and those flowers came from still other seeds, and so on back to—back to—well, back to where?

There's your dog. Where did he come from?

"We got him as a puppy," you say. "And he has a very fine pedigree."

So! That means you know his father's name, and maybe his grandfather's. But how about before that?

One thing you can be sure of. Your dog's grandfather was once a puppy too, and he had a father, and a grandfather, and so

13

PAINTING BY HARRY ANDERSON

is is a wonderful world, full of interesting
ngs. How we should like to know how
ngs began—the beautiful trees and flowers,
winding streams, and the happy birds.

on back to—back to—well, back to when?

Then there's the rooster that's crowing all the time in the neighbor's yard. Where did he come from?

"An egg," you say.

Right. But a hen laid that egg, didn't she? Of course she did. And she came from an egg herself not so long ago. And *that* egg was laid by another hen, and so on back to—well, back to what?

Then there's you. Where did you come from?

"Oh," you say, "Mother brought me home from the hospital."

I suppose she did. But Mother was once a little baby herself, wasn't she? And so was her mother, and her grandmother, and her great-grandmother, and so on back to—back to—well, back to whom?

Think of the mountains and the wooded hills, the flowing rivers, and the sand on the seashore—all the wonderful things of nature. Were they always there, just as you see them now? Or did they too have a beginning? And if so, when and how?

Many great men have tried to explain these things. They have come up with all sorts of strange ideas and suggestions, but most of them are far from the truth.

In only one place—the Bible—will you find the true story. If you will open this wonderful Book, you will find that the very first part is called Genesis, meaning "the book of beginnings." Here you will find the answers to your questions about where everything came from.

That reminds me of a little girl I know. Once I asked her which chapter of the Bible she liked best. I thought she would

14

say, "The twenty-third psalm"—the one that begins "The Lord is my shepherd." But no. She said, "The first chapter of Matthew."

"I suppose you like it because it tells about how Jesus was born," I said.

"Oh, no," she said. "I like it because it's all about the begats."

"The what?" I asked.

"The begats," she said.

So we opened her Bible and turned to Matthew 1, and there it was! "Abraham begat Isaac; and Isaac begat Jacob; and Jacob begat Judas," (KJV) and so on.

I asked her if she knew what the verses meant, and she said, "No, but I do like the begats."

I told her it meant that Abraham had a little boy, and Isaac had a little boy, and Jacob had a little boy, and so on, but I think she still liked the begats best.

Then I told her that if the verses were put the other way around, they would read, "And Jacob had a daddy, and Isaac had a daddy, and Abraham had a daddy," and so on.

She liked that better, but wondered how far back the story goes. I told her what Luke says about it.

In his third chapter, verse 34, Luke picks up the story at Abraham and carries it back further and further. He tells us that Abraham was the son of Terah, "the son of Nahor, the son of Serug," and so on. Such strange names, but they were names of real boys in the long, long ago.

Having told us the names of Abraham's great-grandpa and

great-great-grandpa, and so on, Luke says that Enos was the son of Seth. Seth was "the son of Adam," who was—how very, very wonderful!—who was "the son of God."

There the story ends, and it ends there because it cannot go any farther. It goes clear back to God and stops.

And that's where you go back to. And daddy. And mamma. And everybody's daddy and mamma. Everybody's grandpa and grandma. Everybody's great-grandpa and great-grandma. They all go back across the years, across the centuries, to God.

Not to a monkeylike creature, not to a tiny tadpole in the sea, but to the great and glorious God who made the world and people. And that's exactly what we read in the first words of the first chapter in the Bible, "In the beginning God." ✐

How Everything Began

(Genesis 1:2-6)

MANY years ago I read a story about a boy who picked up a strange little object in the street. It was shaped like a horseshoe and had a mysterious name written on it. The boy tried to pronounce the name, but failed. He tried again and again.

Then one day he said the word a different way, and the object began to grow in his hand. It became bigger and bigger, until at last the horseshoe was as big as a doorway. He stepped through it and found himself in a foreign country, far across the sea.

Using his horseshoe, the boy visited all sorts of strange places. One day he thought he would like to see how people lived long ago. As he whispered the magic word to the horseshoe, he said he would like to visit Rome in the days of the caesars—and, presto, there he was!

Of course someone just made up this story, but it does give us an idea. Would you like to go back and see what the world was like at the very beginning of time? You would? All right.

Let's imagine an archway that we can pass through and travel back across the years.

Steady. Careful. Now we are going through it. Everything around us is fading away. Chairs, table, carpet, TV, are all disappearing. Faces are growing dim. Lights are going out. It is getting darker and darker.

Swiftly we speed back across the years. It's like being in a rocket. We streak over hundreds and thousands of years in a moment. Past the time when Jesus lived on earth. Past the

18

PAINTING BY RUSSELL HARLAN

time of David. Past the time of Abraham. Past the time of Noah. Past the time of Adam.

Oh, dear, how dark it is! We can't see anything. All about us is pitch black. Not a glimmer of light anywhere. Not the tiniest candle. Not the faintest star. Only darkness and night. But we can *hear* something. It is the swishing, gurgling sound that water makes, just as we have heard many times at the seashore or when boating on a lake.

Water. And darkness.

As the Bible says, "darkness was over the surface of the deep."

At once we realize we are not alone. Somebody is here. We know it. We feel it. Amid the darkness, the emptiness, the loneliness, God is here. The Spirit of God is moving "over the waters." God is looking upon the world He has created, planning what He will do with it.

Suddenly, from somewhere—we cannot tell where—we hear a voice. Musical, strong, deep, unlike any voice we have heard before, it commands the darkness to give place to light.

Instantly the darkness vanishes. We can see again. Not very far. Only a few feet, a few yards perhaps, because all around us is a thick mist. But how wonderful is the light after the dark!

We see no blue sky or bright sunshine, just a kind of brilliant fog, and under it, water, water, everywhere. We see no land, just this vast, restless, heaving ocean. Not a man or a woman, not a boy or a girl, not a bird or an animal. No, not even a fish in the sea. Only light in the mist and on the water.

"God saw that the light was good, and he separated the light from the darkness. God called the light 'day' and the darkness he called 'night.' And there was evening, and there was morning—the first day."

The first day! The very beginning of everything in this old world. The beginning of time. The beginning of history. The beginning of all human happiness and sorrow. On this day the great and loving Creator drew near this dark little speck in space and said, "Let there be light!"

Great Preparations

(Genesis 1:6-10)

AS THE light of earth's first day fades into night, something strange and wonderful begins to happen. Silently, mysteriously, the heavy, moisture-laden mist close to the ocean begins to rise. All night and all the next morning it goes up, up, up, until it becomes a beautiful fleecy-white covering high above the world. Between it and the water below, clear, fresh air forms the atmosphere. The Bible calls it "expanse" or "firmament."

"And God said, 'Let there be an expanse between the waters to separate water from water.' So God made the expanse and separated the water under the expanse from the water above it. And it was so. God called the expanse 'sky.' And there was evening, and there was morning—the second day."

Perhaps you wonder why God took one whole day of Creation week to make something invisible, like the atmosphere, when He gave another whole day to making the fish in the sea, and another to making the animals. Things are not unimportant just because they cannot be seen. What God did on the

second day was of very great importance. Everything else depended on it. You see, He was planning to make a beautiful world full of animals, and they would all need air to breathe. He planned to make birds too, and they would need air in which to fly. Without air their wings would be useless. He was also about to make trees and plants and flowers, and He knew they would need nitrogen to help them grow.

So He mixed nitrogen with oxygen and a few other gases, and made air. He used just the right amount of each gas. Not too much and not too little. Had He mixed in too little oxygen, all His creatures would have suffocated. Had He mixed in too much, one spark would have set the world on fire.

God had yet another reason for making the air first. It would divide the waters "above"—that is, in the clouds—from the waters "under"—or in the ocean. The air was to be a barrier between them. Without it, raindrops from a mile-high cloud would have hit the earth like machine-gun bullets. One heavy downpour would have just about destroyed everything.

How wise of God to make the atmosphere right after He made light and before He made anything else! To have done otherwise would have been a dreadful mistake. His whole lovely plan might have been spoiled, but God does not make mistakes.

When we think of how He made the world, we will feel like saying with the apostle Paul, "Oh, the depth of the riches of the wisdom and knowledge of God! How unsearchable his judgments, and his paths beyond tracing out!"*

Now earth's second day is ending. The beautiful white cloud is changing color. Shot through with gold, orange, red, purple, it slowly vanishes in darkness as night draws on.

Two days have gone, two out of six. All that we can see is the ocean, the great endless ocean. No land, no living creature. Nothing but water. North, south, east, west, only water, water, water, the restless waves rolling on, on, on to nowhere.

In the darkness of the third evening it seems as though God has done nothing but lift the moisture-laden mist from the ocean. But He is not impatient. He is not hurried. He knows that all is now ready for the next great step in creation.

Listen! He is speaking again: "And God said, 'Let the water under the sky be gathered to one place, and let dry ground appear.' "

Suddenly the great ocean begins to boil. There is a mighty

shaking and shuddering as out of the depths rise the first pieces of land. Continents and islands swiftly take shape. Mountains and hills push upward as water drains from their sides in foaming cascades.

What a night! What a day!

As morning dawns on the third day and light shines through the radiant clouds once more, it reveals no longer only an ocean, but great stretches of dry land. It is beautiful land, with lakes, rivers, and waterfalls, and beyond it all, the sea.

How very wonderful! Yesterday only an ocean. Today a beautiful world. Now we know for sure that God has a great plan in mind. He is building something, building a home for somebody He loves.

* Romans 11:33

Birthday of a World

(Genesis 1:9-13)

IT IS still early on the third day of Creation week. During a very great earthquake, land has mysteriously risen from the ocean. Islands of all sizes and shapes have appeared. We can see majestic mountains, rolling hills, and lovely beaches where before we saw only sea.

Yet something is missing. The land looks dark and barren except for bright, glittering patches here and there where precious metals lie on the surface. Not a tree or a bush or a blade of grass grows anywhere. Surely God does not intend for anyone to live in a place like this!

Wait a minute. It is too soon to judge. Listen! The same wonderful voice that said, "Let there be light," is speaking again. "Let the land produce vegetation: seed-bearing plants and trees on the land that bear fruit with seed in it, according to their various kinds."

Now look. What a transformation! The hills have turned a vivid green. From one side to the other they are covered with grass, bushes, trees. Look at the mountains! See those glorious pines, cedars, redwoods, reaching up the sides of the highest peaks.

And the fields. What beauty! Look at all the flowers! Masses of them, of all kinds and colors. They look like a living carpet spread over the whole countryside. Buttercups and daisies, poppies and marigolds, bluebells and daffodils, hollyhocks and snapdragons, geraniums and delphiniums, orchids and begonias, roses and lilacs. How did God think of so many? How marvelously He made them all, each with its own delicate design, its own special coloring and fragrance!

"The land produced vegetation: plants bearing seed according to their kinds and trees bearing fruit with seed in it according to their kinds. And God saw that it was good."

It must have been very, very good, with God as the designer and maker of it all. I like to think that He enjoyed Himself making all these plants and flowers and trees, each one different from all the others. Then He gave them the power to reproduce, all "according to their kinds," through all time to come.

God seems to have been especially interested in the fruit trees. With what care He made the apple trees, the plum trees, the pear trees, the orange trees, the lemon trees, the avocado trees, and all the rest! I think I can see Him moving from one beautiful tree to another, perhaps even tasting the fruit, saying to Himself, "They'll like this. I'm sure they will. And this . . . and this."

For God was not thinking of Himself, but of a special man and woman. The beginning of a family who at the moment existed only in His mind, but who soon would be real, living beings. A family to whom He was planning to give all this beauty and loveliness, all this wealth of treasure and delight.

All the gold, silver, and precious stones that sparkled and glittered amid the grass and the flowers were for them. All the generous provision of nuts, fruits, and grains was for them. All the glory of this wonderful new world—all was for *them*, to make them happy, to cause them to turn with loving adoration and thankfulness to their Creator.

The world was nearly ready for them. Nearly, but not quite. God had to do a few more things.

"And there was evening, and there was morning—the third day."

The First Rays of Sunshine

(Genesis 1:14-19)

I N THREE short days the dark, water-covered globe has been changed into a Paradise of beauty.

Driven up from the ocean depths by some mighty, unseen force, land has appeared. Just as wonderfully and suddenly, the new continents and islands have been covered with grass and flowers, shrubs and trees, of every shape and size and color.

Now the fourth day has come. Night has passed. Dawn is breaking. From the bright clouds above the atmosphere, a gentle light makes God's work of yesterday seem more beautiful than ever.

But look! Something is happening. Up there. In the cloud cover. It is breaking up. See! Beyond it is a bright light, a ball of fire. What can it be? It is the sun! Already its first warm rays are sweeping over the lovely landscape, making it more and more like a gorgeous fairyland. Flowers are turning eagerly toward the shining giant ball of fire. Ferns lift their fronds and trees their branches in joyous welcome.

29

What a beautiful world God made, when He created the green fields of grass, the lovely ponds, the graceful trees, the pretty flowers, and everything that was pleasant to the eyes.

For the first time all the beauty of the newly made world is open to the full view of the inhabitants of heaven. It is as though God had drawn back a curtain that they might see what He had done and enjoy His handiwork with Him. From far away comes the sound of wondrous music as "the morning stars" sing together and "all the angels" shout for joy.

Around the sun a circle of blue gets larger and larger as the cloud cover dissolves. It is the sky, the lovely blue sky, which, reflected in the lakes and seas below, makes them the same color as itself.

Hanging there in the sky is the pale moon, waiting for nightfall to take its place as the light of the world.

"And God said, 'Let there be lights in the expanse of the sky to separate the day from the night, and let them serve as signs to mark seasons and days and years, and let them be lights in the expanse of the sky to give light on the earth.' And it was so. God made two great lights—the greater light to govern the day and the lesser light to govern the night. He also made the stars.

"God set them in the expanse of the sky to give light on the

30

earth, to govern the day and the night, and to separate light from darkness. And God saw that it was good."

It *was* good—very good, and very necessary. For without the light and warmth of the sun many of the plants and trees that God had made could not have lasted long. He knew this, and in His wisdom made plans for the care of everything. He knew too that the animals He was about to make would love the sunshine and that they could never keep healthy and strong without it. His new family would love it too and need it just as much. For their sake, most of all, those first rays shone upon the earth.

In all this God was thinking not only of today and tomorrow but of many days to come. The world He was making was not to be just a toy to play with, which He would toss away when He was tired of it. He was building for eternity. That is why He planned that the sun and moon should mark the passing not only of days but also of the "seasons" and the "years," many seasons and many years. If the family He was about to make should choose to love and obey Him, they could enjoy this glorious land for ever and ever.

Although His family was not yet made, I feel sure that there was hidden within the heart of God the hope that all their years would be happy, time without end; that the sun might never mark a day of sorrow or the moon a night of pain.

"And there was evening, and there was morning—the fourth day."

Out of the Silence—a Song

(Genesis 1:20-23)

BEAUTIFUL beyond words is the world that God has made, but it is a silent and empty world.

As morning dawns on the fifth day not a sound is heard anywhere except the sighing of the wind in the trees and the gentle splashing of the waves on the beaches. No lions roar, no elephants trumpet in the forest. Not even one little frog croaks in the fern-lined pools. Not a dog barks, not a coyote howls, not a crow caws. There is no sound of a human voice. No shout of a boy, no laughter of a little girl. How quiet it must have been!

But God does not want an empty world or a silent world. He is making it to be inhabited. All His great preparations of the first day, the second day, the third day, the fourth day, are to make ready a home for a multitude of living creatures.

So now, as the sun shines warm and bright upon the lovely flower-covered countryside and the deep-blue sea beyond, God moves into action again.

"And God said, 'Let the water teem with living creatures,

32

and let birds fly above the earth across the expanse of the sky.'

"So God created the great creatures of the sea and every living and moving thing with which the water teems, according to their kinds, and every winged bird according to its kind. And God saw that it was good.

"God blessed them and said, 'Be fruitful and increase in number and fill the water in the seas, and let the birds increase on the earth.' "

What a wonderful day that was! Don't you wish you really could have been there? I do. I would love to have watched God make the first goldfish, the first silver salmon, and send the first great whale surging through the sea like a giant submarine.

I am sure He enjoyed Himself making all those fish, but how did He think of many different kinds? The big fat porpoise and the little brown trout, the marvelous blue sailfish and the tiny minnow, the sunfish and the starfish, the swordfish and the cuttlefish, the crabs and the shrimps, the lobsters and the eels.

I cannot begin to think of them all, but God thought of them all. He designed them and made them, all in one day, all different, all with the power to live and move and get oxygen—under water! How wonderful is our Creator! How we should honor and adore Him!

Making a thousand varieties of fish all at once was not enough. On this same day He made the birds too. He designed the wingspread of the eagle, the gorgeous plumage of the peacock, the brilliant colors of the parrot, and the mimicking skill of the mockingbird.

Just look at them! What a marvelous sight! Hundreds and thousands of birds of every size and shape and color rise from the earth. See them flapping their wings, swooping up and down here and there, in the full joy of living!

And what is that? Listen! The silence is broken at last. From everywhere comes the sound of music. The birds are singing! The air is filled with their lovely songs.

From far up in the blue comes the sweet warble of the skylark, and from deep in the forest the lovely song of the nightingale and the cheery trill of a canary. Nearby, sparrows are twittering, doves are cooing, and meadowlarks, killdeers, and whippoorwills are pouring forth their songs in praise to Him who made them. What wonderful harmony!

"And there was evening, and there was morning—the fifth day."

34

The Animals Appear

(Genesis 1:24, 25)

FOR a few short hours the birds had the world all to themselves. They flew happily through the air, perched on the branches of the trees, and walked or waddled through the flower-strewn meadows. No doubt they thought—if birds can think—what a lovely place God had made for them.

But God had not made this marvelous wonderland just for them. Early on the morning of the sixth day a loud roar shook a forest. Chirping and twittering, birds exploded into the air from nearby trees. Curious to see what the noise was about, they flew back and saw a great yellow creature with a fine, strong face, a long, hairy mane, and a bearing like a king. It was the first lion to roam the earth.

Look over there! What a strange animal, with four long legs, a big, long neck, and such a funny face! A giraffe, of course! Ambling by with its head high in the air, it almost knocks the smallest birds out of the trees.

And what is this huge creature with legs like tree trunks,

big flapping ears, and little tiny eyes? On the end of its nose is a long tube, which it tosses this way and that, sometimes even putting it into its curious little mouth. Oh, dear! What fun God must have had making the elephant!

Here come some horses, perhaps black or brown. They gallop gracefully by with their heads tossing and their feet going clippety-clop, clippety-clop, in perfect rhythm. Now a couple of zebras, with strange markings on their coats, trot past. Here come two leopards, with spots all over them; a crocodile, waddling on its little short legs; a hippopotamus, trudging by with its huge mouth open; a camel, with its humps; a deer, with its antlers; a bear, with its long, shaggy coat.

What a procession! And to think that God designed and made all these creatures in such a short time! Yet this is not half the story. Not only did He make all the big animals, but He made the tiny ones too.

Look there! A little dog barks and scampers about as all dogs have done from that day to this. A cat walks by with stately steps. A monkey swings from branch to branch. A chipmunk makes funny faces. A gopher burrows fast to make a home for itself in the earth. A chameleon changes color to match the sun-spotted leaves around it. A squirrel, with a big, bushy tail, scurries around looking for something to bury.

All these animals God created in a single day! This is too wonderful for us to understand. Just think! Every one of these

marvelous creatures was not only made alive but was made to see, hear, smell, taste, and eat, just like you and me. More than that, each one was given the power to reproduce, to make baby animals just like itself.

You can draw animals on paper. You can make animals of clay. But you cannot make even one of your animals live. You can't make them walk or run or eat, can you? No, indeed. It's just as well, for if you could, what would Mother do with all of them running about the house? And how would she feed so many?

No, we cannot make animals that live. We can't make even a toad or a mosquito, but God can. And God did. In His creative mind every animal, every insect, had its beginning. At the sound of His voice they sprang forth from the earth.

"And God said, 'Let the land produce living creatures according to their kinds: livestock, creatures that move along the ground, and wild animals, each according to its kind.' And it was so. God made the wild animals according to their kinds, the livestock according to their kinds, and all the creatures that move along the ground according to their kinds. And God saw that it was good."

God was pleased with His work. "It was good," and He was happy. His creatures were happy too, and peaceful. Yet Creation was not complete. Something was missing. The most important thing of all remained to be done. God had left it till the last.

God Makes a Man

(Genesis 1:26-2:7)

HAVE you ever planned a wonderful surprise for Mother's birthday? I'm sure you have. You may have bought something for her from the store or made it all by yourself. A cake, maybe, or some candy, a painting, or some needlework. Whatever it was, I know you could hardly wait for the day to come when you could give it to her.

Something like this thrill must have been in God's heart on that sixth day of Creation week. That day was going to be a birthday too, and He knew it. All that week He had been getting the present ready, and what a present it was! A whole world! A beautiful, beautiful world. A world full of treasures—gold and silver and precious stones. A world full of food—nuts, fruit, grains, and pure, sparkling water. A world full of loveliness—trees and ferns and flowers. A world full of marvelous living creatures—birds and fish and animals of every kind and color to study, to play with, to laugh at.

← PAINTING BY VERNON NYE

Before God made man He had everything ready for his happiness. A beautiful garden was prepared for him to live in. Then with loving care He created him in His own image.

During the time that God was preparing this present, He was thinking about the wonderful new family He was soon to create. He was saying to Himself, "I hope they will enjoy it; I hope it will make them happy. I hope that they will notice all the things I have done to please them and that they will love Me in return."

At last, when everything is ready, and God has done everything He can think of to make the world a Paradise, He says: " 'Let us make man in our image, in our likeness, and let them rule over the fish of the sea and the birds of the air, over the livestock, over all the earth, and over all the creatures that move along the ground.'

"So God created man in his own image, in the image of God he created him; male and female he created them."

"In his own image!" Like God! How very, very wonderful!

God might have said, "Let us make man like a monkey." But He didn't. He might have said, "Let us make man like a lion, only bigger and stronger." But He didn't. He might have said, "Let us make man like an eagle, giving him wings to fly over the highest mountain." But He didn't. Instead He chose to make man like Himself. He could have given him no greater honor, shown him no greater love.

"The Lord God formed the man from the dust of the ground." "Formed" him. With infinite wisdom, infinite patience, infinite tenderness, He molds the noble head, the kind face, the strong body. He builds into him something

40

more wonderful than television—the power to see. Something more wonderful than radio—the power to hear. Something more wonderful than radar—the power to think and talk and remember. Best of all, God makes it possible for man to love and laugh and worship.

Finally the task is completed. With infinite gentleness God puts the last finishing touches on His masterpiece. There on the earth from which he had been made lies man—the very first man. He lies silent and still like some beautiful statue, waiting for the gift of life.

And God "breathed into his nostrils the breath of life, and the man became a living being."

How near God comes to him! So very, very close! The mouth of God touches the mouth of man! Perhaps, who knows, God kisses him. Perhaps, too, tears of love fill His eyes as He bends low over the wonderful creature He has made. This man is so like Himself, so dear to His heart.

God whispers to him, gently, tenderly, lovingly, breathing into him His own wonderful life. Adam, for that is his name, awakens. His eyes wide with wonder, he looks up into the face of his Maker.

Adam's First Meal

(Genesis 1:28-30)

LEAPING to his feet, Adam looks around him at the beautiful world in which he finds himself. I wonder what he thought and what he said.

Of course he had nobody to talk to except God and himself—and the animals. That some of them were nearby goes without saying, for animals are always full of curiosity, aren't they? I can almost see a little dog licking his hand and a cat brushing past his leg, hoping to be noticed, and maybe a horse nosing in to be petted.

Other animals come from all directions—perhaps a lion and an elephant, a bear and a beaver, a big fat panda and a saucy little chipmunk. They are all so friendly, and each one gazes wide-eyed at the magnificent creature before them. Somehow they seem to recognize in him their leader and master. As he strides over the soft, green grass, they follow him gladly, leaping and frisking about in pride and joy.

Happy cries of welcome fill the meadows and forests as the grand procession moves on its way over hill and dale, by shady

43

How happy Adam must have been to have all the animals love to come to him. It must have been fun to name them all, for he knew just what to call them when he saw them.

pool, tinkling stream, and sandy lakeshore. Adam pauses often to marvel at some fresh wonder of Creation, perhaps a tall, graceful tree or radiantly beautiful flower. As he pauses, more animals appear from the forest, while birds swoop low to see what is going on.

Instinct tells them that this tall, handsome being, with the flashing eyes and kingly bearing, has been given "rule over the fish of the sea and the birds of the air and over every living creature that moves on the ground."

No heart feels any fear. Adam is not afraid of the tiger that follows close at his heels, nor is the tiger afraid of him. Without thought of harm, a deer plays with a leopard. Antelopes, buffaloes, camels, zebras, and kangaroos graze together in perfect peace and harmony.

Seeing the animals eat reminds Adam that he is hungry. But where is his food? He notices some purple grapes hanging from a vine, then some bright red berries, and again clusters of nuts on the trees. Could these be his food?

As he wonders which he should take he hears God's voice saying to him, "I give you every seed-bearing plant on the face of the whole earth and every tree that has fruit with seed in it. They will be yours for food."

So he may take his choice. They are all for him. But with so many lovely things, he finds it hard to decide which to eat first. A banana, perhaps? Or an apple, or maybe some almonds, or pecans, or a bunch of grapes? Dear, oh, dear, what a problem!

Just what he ate first we do not know, but of one

thing we may be certain — Adam's first meal must have been the finest anyone has ever eaten. Every item on the menu was fresh from the Creator's hand, brought into existence but three short days before. How tasty, how delicious, it must have been! Don't you wish you could have shared it with him?

Did it ever occur to you how wonderful it was that God created the grass *before* He made the animals to eat it? That He made the fruit trees and nut trees before He made man, who would need these things for food? That He designed trees and vines and grasses to draw from the earth just those very minerals and nutrients that living creatures need to keep them alive? How carefully, how marvelously He planned every detail of this glorious new world of His!

It is now late in the afternoon of the sixth day. Already the sun is sinking toward the western horizon. God's work of Creation is almost over. Everything He intended to do to make a perfect home for Adam has been done. Everything, that is, but one.

He has created the earth out of nothing. He has divided the land from the sea. He has covered the mountains and the hills with gorgeous trees and flowers. He has made the birds, the fishes, and the animals. Crowning all, He has made Adam "in his own image." Adam, His masterpiece, the supreme object of His love, for whom all this beauty and abundance has been provided.

Yet one thing more remains to be done — one last beautiful blessing to bestow. It is the sweetest, loveliest act of all Creation.

Fairest Creature of Creation

(Genesis 1:31; 2:18, 20-23)

AS ADAM watches the animals lying in the warm sunshine or playing happily in the meadows, he soon notices that they are in pairs. Every animal has a mate. Beside the majestic lion strides a sleek and slender lioness. Behind the antlered stag moves a graceful doe. With the powerful bull is a gentle cow. Near the tiger is a tigress. Close to the bear is a she-bear. Not far from Mr. Rabbit is Mrs. Rabbit, and it is so with the giraffes and zebras, the rhinos and the antelopes, the opossums and the squirrels. Only Adam is alone.

Of course, the animals are as friendly to him as they can be. When he calls to them they stop and look at him with their great, big, wondering eyes, but they cannot say a word in return. The little dog seems to understand him best, and it is clear that it wants ever so badly to speak. But all it can do is wiggle and jump about and bark and wag its tail.

Many times Adam must have wondered why he had no mate. Perhaps he began to search for one. Perhaps, out of the

47

← PAINTING BY RUSSELL HARLAN
Like a great master artist, God put the finishing touch on creation by making a woman, the world's first mother, the most lovely of all His creatures, whom Adam named Eve.

ache in his heart, he called and called, hoping that someone like him might hear his voice and answer. Perhaps he half expected to see some beautiful creature walking through the forest toward him to be his special friend and companion. But no one came.

As he lies on the grass and thinks about these things, he grows more and more lonely. The earth is so beautiful, the animals *so* friendly and amusing, but he has nobody to talk to, nobody with whom he can share his thoughts. Nobody, that is, except God.

Suddenly Adam begins to feel very sleepy. *This is strange,* he thinks. He has never felt like this before. What can be happening to him? He tries to stay awake, but it is no use. Moment by moment he becomes sleepier and sleepier, until at last he can keep his eyes open no longer. The earth, the flowers, the trees, the animals—all fade away and are forgotten as he falls into deep slumber.

Now God draws near to him, as near as He had been a little while before when He had breathed into his nostrils the breath of life. With one swift touch of His gentle, creative hands He removes a rib from the sleeping form before Him, closing up the wound with infinite skill.

"Then the Lord God made a woman from the rib he had taken out of the man."

What a strange thing for God to do! He made the sun, the moon, the stars, by saying, "Let there be lights in the expanse of the sky." He made all the fish and birds by saying, "Let the water teem with living creatures, and let birds fly above the

48

earth across the expanse of the sky." Why didn't He say, "Let there be a woman"? And why, after making Adam, the most marvelous creature in His wonderful world, did He take a rib from his perfect body to make his life companion?

God must have had a good reason for acting this way. I like to think it was because He wanted Adam to know that his wife was truly part of him, so that he would always treat her as he would himself. The Bible tells us that God made Eve to be "a helper suitable for" Adam. Our word "helpmate" comes from this idea, and what a lovely thought it is! Eve was to stand by his side, always helping him, working with him, planning with him, and sharing life's joys with him.

Let us watch God at work again. Of Adam's rib we are told He "made" a woman. Even as He "formed" man of the dust of the ground, so now, with infinite wisdom and skill, He fashions the one who is to become the mother of the whole human race. How perfectly He molds the features of her lovely face! How gracefully He arranges her long, flowing hair! With what loving thought He places within her mind and heart all the tenderness, all the gentleness, all the sweetness, all the endless store of love He wants every woman to have!

In less time than it takes to tell the fairest creature of all Creation stands before her Creator. Her eyes sparkle with the joy of life, and a tender smile gives her pretty face a beauty beyond compare. Now, slowly and gracefully, she takes her first few steps as God brings her "to the man." Wonderingly she looks down at the sleeping figure before her. Who can this be?

Dreaming perhaps of the companion he hopes to meet someday, somewhere, in this wonderful world God has given him, Adam stirs and opens his eyes. Oh, wonder of wonders! There before him stands someone more beautiful than he had dared to hope for. A being so special, so noble, so altogether lovely that he can scarcely believe that she is real.

Looking into her bright, kind, understanding eyes, he knows at once that this is his mate. This is the dear companion for whom he has longed. "The man said, 'This is now bone of my bones and flesh of my flesh; she shall be called "woman," for she was taken out of man.' "

It is love at first sight. Instantly both seem to know that they belong to each other. Eagerly they link hands and walk away together. As king and queen of the glorious new earth, they wander through the flower-filled fields, over the tree-studded hills, and down by the wave-swept shore. Together they explore the wonders of God's Creation and marvel at the glory of His power.

Meanwhile, not far away, silently watching over them in tender love, smiling at their perfect happiness, is God Himself. His joy is complete in theirs.

PART TWO

Stories of

Eden

and

the Fall

(Genesis 2:8-5:27)

Man's Garden Home

(Genesis 2:8-19)

SOMEWHERE in the wonderful, beautiful world that He had created "the Lord God had planted a garden in the east, in Eden." There He put the man and woman He had made.

Have you ever planted a garden? It's exciting, isn't it! Especially in the springtime when you sow seeds and wait for the little green shoots to come up. How thrilling it is when the flowers begin to bloom, the corn ripens, and the cabbages and heads of lettuce get fat and hard and ready to eat!

When God planted the Garden of Eden, He didn't need to plant seeds. As Creator He could make full-grown trees and bushes appear immediately all in the right place, just where He wanted them. He could say, I want a cluster of tall cedars here and a grove of silver birches there, and they would appear at the sound of His voice. He could call for a hill to be covered with pines, another with redwoods, and another with oaks, and it would be so. He could call for a valley to be carpeted with yellow buttercups, another with scarlet poppies, and another

53

Adam and Eve loved each other and everything God had given them. They were happy tending this beautiful garden so full of delightful vines, fruit trees, and fragrant flowers.

with sweet-smelling hyacinths, and it would be so.

How glorious the garden home must have been that He planted especially for Adam and Eve. We can only imagine its splendor as we think of some of nature's wonderlands that we know and love today.

Notice that God did not build them a palace, though He had made them king and queen of the world. He did not make some fine stone house for them, with marble floors and electric lighting, though He had given them silver and gold in abundance. Instead He made them a home among the trees and flowers.

For walls this home had palms and firs and maples. Its floor was the soft, sweet-smelling earth, gorgeously carpeted with bluebells, marigolds, and primroses. For the roof it had the spreading branches of trees. Above them, in the glorious dome of heaven, the sun gave light in the daytime, and the moon and the stars gave light at night.

Adam and Eve didn't need shelter, for it didn't rain or storm in that far-off day when the world was born. Instead, "streams came up from the earth and watered the whole surface of the ground."

Adam and Eve's first home had no bedroom as we think of bedrooms. They slept in cozy, moss-covered nooks among the bushes, or on flower-covered meadows beside rippling streams. Their living room was a hillside overlooking some enchanting bay or sandy, lakeside cove. Their music room was among the

trees, where the birds trilled their lovely songs. Their kitchen
and cupboards were the fruit-bearing vines and bushes, always
loaded with good things to eat.

No home ever built has been so beautiful, so peaceful, so
perfect, as this glorious garden home that the Lord God planted
in Eden in the long ago.

How happy Adam and Eve must have been as, hand in
hand, they hurried from one lovely scene to another! I can
almost hear Eve crying out, "O Adam, look at this pretty
flower. And this, and this! How good they smell! What a
wonderful place to live!"

Walking eagerly along, they come suddenly upon two remarkable trees that are different from all the others they have
seen, and both are loaded with brilliantly colored fruit.

As Adam and Eve admire this new and wonderful sight, God
draws near. He tells them that they are now in the very center of
their garden home and that one of these trees is the tree of life
and the other the tree of the knowledge of good and evil.

"And the Lord God commanded the man, 'You are free to
eat from any tree in the garden; but you must not eat from the
tree of the knowledge of good and evil, for when you eat of it
you will surely die.' "

Die? they wonder. What does God mean? And why has He
planted a tree in the garden from which they must not eat? Still
wondering, they go on their happy way together as the sun sinks
lower toward the horizon.

What a day it has been! At dawn the animals came leaping out of the earth at the call of their Creator. Then He made man in His own image, in His own likeness. At last, with infinite wisdom, love, and understanding, He fashioned His most beautiful and perfect work, a woman.

Now this wonderful day is drawing to a close. Shadows are lengthening, and birds are twittering in the trees. The animals are settling down for their first night in their new home.

Gazing westward at the blazing glory of the sunset, Adam and Eve stand awestruck as the sky is filled with wondrous colors. A new beauty glows from every tree and flower. What can be happening? they wonder. Is their beautiful world coming to an end so soon? God whispers to them, "This is just the sunset; watch for the glory of the dawn."

"God saw all that he had made, and it was very good." It was. Very, very good. The earth, the sea, the trees, the flowers, the animals, are all as perfect as God could make them. Now this pair of happy human beings, so stately, so beautiful, so sweetly innocent, were bowing in reverent worship of their Maker. What more could even God desire?

Creation is complete. God's work is done. He has finished His work of love. No wonder heaven rings with His praise. Once more "the morning stars" sing together and "all the angels of God" shout for joy.

A Day to Remember

(Genesis 2:2, 3)

AS THE sun goes down on the sixth day of Creation week a wonderful calm falls over the whole countryside. Gradually the twittering of the birds in the forest grows fainter and fainter until at last everything falls silent. The stars come out, and all nature is bathed in brilliant moonlight.

Somewhere in the garden, perhaps in some lovely mossy meadow, sit Adam and Eve, marveling at the beauty of the evening as they had at the glory of the day. Suddenly, out of the silence, comes a voice—tender, kind, and musical. They know at once it is God's voice. Perhaps this is when God told them about the Sabbath. He must have told them. Otherwise, how else could they have known that their first complete day on the earth was to be a holy day?

God must have told them, too, how He had created everything around them in six days. Now, on the seventh day, He and they would rest together. The Bible says that "by the seventh day God had finished the work he had been doing; so

57

on the seventh day he rested from all his work. And God blessed the seventh day and made it holy, because on it he rested from all the work of creating that he had done."

God did not rest because He was tired, for God doesn't get tired. Rather He rested because His work of Creation was finished. The world was as perfect as He could make it. He could do nothing more to make it serve His purpose better.

He rested, too, because He wanted to set an example for Adam and Eve and their children to follow. You see, God not only "rested" on this day, but He also "blessed" it and "made it holy." This tells us clearly that He was thinking not of Himself but of His earthly children.

He blessed the Sabbath so it would be a blessing to *them*. He set it apart as a holy day not for Himself, but for *them*. Even now, six thousand years later, all who keep the seventh day holy find a blessing in it that others never know! In some wonderful way the peace and happiness of heaven come into their hearts as they follow the plan God gave to Adam and Eve in the beginning.

And now, once more we see them on that quiet evening in the long ago. They listen reverently to their Creator's voice as He tells them that their very first full day upon the earth is to be a holy day, spent together with Him. They are perfectly happy. In the morning the rising sun wakens them from their first night's sleep. God Himself leads them through the beautiful garden He has made to be their home.

Perhaps He shows them some of the marvelous secrets of Creation. As they stop to admire some beautiful tree or lovely

58

flowering shrub, He explains how the plants draw their food from the soil. He describes how the sap rises through the trunk and out into the branches, the twigs, the leaves, the flowers.

Perhaps He tells them how a beautiful white lily grows from a little brown bulb, how a small blue-speckled egg becomes a yellow canary, how a tiny seed inside an apple grows to be another apple tree.

Maybe He explains how a bee gathers honey, how a spider spins its web, and how white milk comes from a red cow that eats green grass. Perhaps, too, He tells them the secret of flight—how an eagle can fly above the mountains and a hummingbird hover like a helicopter.

We do not know exactly what they talked about that day, but it must have been thrilling to walk through creation with the Creator. Again and again as Adam and Eve saw the beauty and perfection of everything around them, they must have exclaimed, "Great and marvelous are your deeds, Lord God Almighty!" [1]

That first day of rest and worship and fellowship with God was a very, very happy day. Adam and Eve remembered it and talked about it all their lives.

God wants every Sabbath to be as nearly like that first Sabbath as possible. That's why, when He gave us the Ten Commandments on Mount Sinai, He said, "Remember the Sabbath day by keeping it holy. Six days you shall labor and do all your work, but the seventh day is a Sabbath to the Lord your God. On it you shall not do any work, neither you, nor your son or daughter, nor your manservant or maidservant, nor your

59

animals, nor the alien within your gates." He added, so we wouldn't forget, "For in six days the Lord made the heavens and the earth, the sea, and all that is in them, but he rested on the seventh day. Therefore the Lord blessed the Sabbath day and made it holy." [2]

Thousands of years after that first Sabbath in the Garden of Eden, God was still thinking about it. He could not forget it, and never will. Because it was so happy, so beautiful, so truly blessed, He wants everyone else to remember it too.

Every Sabbath can be like that one if we want it to be. It can be just as happy, just as beautiful, just as blessed. All we have to do each seventh day is to remember to keep it holy, to walk and talk with God, and to worship Him as the Creator of the heavens and the earth.

[1] Revelation 15:3.
[2] Exodus 20:8-11.

The First Mistake

(Genesis 2:15-3:4)

THOSE first few days that Adam and Eve spent in the Garden of Eden must have been supremely happy. They didn't have a care in the world. Not a single one. How good they felt! How strong, how radiantly healthy! They didn't know what sickness meant. They never had a headache or a toothache. Day after day they woke up from untroubled sleep, refreshed and ready for anything.

Life was glorious, and work was so pleasant and easy it was just like play. All God asked them to do in their lovely garden home was "to work it and take care of it." There were no weeds, or thorns, or thistles to bother them. They didn't have to spend long hours putting up buildings or making clothes. The climate was so warm and delightful that they didn't need any.

As for food, the finest fruits, nuts, and vegetables, full of life-giving vitamins, grew all around them. They could have all they wanted, just for the picking, and they didn't have to do any cooking or wash any dishes!

Adam and Eve's first home was beautiful, peaceful, and

61

happy beyond words. And they could still be living there, if they hadn't made one sad mistake. That mistake, which seemed so small and unimportant at the moment, proved to be the turning point in their lives. Afterward nothing was ever the same again.

It happened this way. One day Eve wanted to take another look at the two wonderful trees with all their brightly colored fruit in the center of the garden. Why, she wondered, had God given one of them such an odd name—"the tree of the knowledge of good and evil"? What did "good" mean? What was "evil"? And why couldn't she eat its fruit? How could it possibly hurt her?

It seemed strange that God, after giving them so much, should not give them everything. Why should He hold back one tree? But Eve didn't think of disobeying Him. Not then.

62

Maybe she told herself that He would explain all about it someday. He probably had some good reason.

As she turns away, perhaps to look at the lovely "tree of life," she is startled to hear someone speaking to her. Who can it be? The only voices she has heard up to now have been God's and Adam's. Now someone else is speaking. Astonished, she looks this way and that, but sees nobody. Then she notices that the voice is coming from a snake. How very remarkable! An animal that can talk! She waits to see if it will speak again.

It does, and its voice is so friendly and pleasing that any fears she may have had disappear. After all, it is rather nice to have someone else to talk to, even though it is only a snake.

Who is this snake? And why is it able to talk?

The Bible tells us that it was "the devil, or Satan, who

leads the whole world astray." * His name had originally been Lucifer, the light bearer. He had once been the leader of the angels in heaven, but he rebelled against God and was thrown out of heaven. Then he came to this earth to take revenge on God by trying to spoil His plans for human happiness.

Of course, Eve didn't know all this. Not then. If she had, she surely would not have listened to him. All she knew was that here was a most unusual creature talking to her in a kindly, gracious voice.

The snake says, "Did God really say, 'You must not eat from any tree in the garden'?"

"Yes," Eve says to him innocently. "God did tell us that we may eat fruit growing on the trees in the garden. But He also said that we must not eat any fruit from the tree in the middle of the garden. We must not touch it, or we will die."

"You will not surely die," the snake says with a sneer, as though nothing of the sort could possibly happen.

Strange! Eve thinks. *This creature is actually saying that God did not tell the truth! How dare he? It isn't right.*

She should have run from the scene, but she didn't. She stayed. She listened. And here she made her first mistake.

Oh, what a lot of sorrow came from it! What a price we pay for lingering near what we know is wrong!

_____
* Revelation 12:9.

The Test of Love

(Genesis 3:5, 6)

A S EVE stands by "the tree of the knowledge of good and evil," listening to the soft-spoken words of the snake, the first doubt enters her mind. God had said that if she ate fruit from this tree she would die. Now the snake was saying that she wouldn't die. Who was right? Could it be that God had not told the truth?

As she thinks this over, the snake follows with another idea. He says, "God knows that when you eat of it your eyes will be opened, and you will be like God, knowing good and evil." He is suggesting that God has been unfair to her and Adam, that He is holding back something that belongs to them. There is a sly hint, too, that God is jealous of them, afraid that they might become as wise as He.

It was very wicked and mean of the snake to say such things when God had been so good to Adam and Eve, but Satan is like that. He is always working against God, always suggesting unkind and hateful things, always trying to make trouble and separate friends.

Satan's suggestion about "knowing good and evil" makes Eve curious. Up to this moment she has not known anything about evil. She may even have asked herself what the snake meant by the word. What was evil like? She thinks it might be good to find out.

That is always dangerous. It's the first step along the path to trouble and sorrow. We always need to be on guard against suggestions to try some wrong thing in order to learn how it feels or how it tastes. We shouldn't want to know evil. We are far better off without that kind of knowledge. No one has to put a finger into a bottle of ink to know it's black.

Little by little Eve falls for Satan's tricks. First she begins to doubt God's word. Next it seems that it won't matter much if she disobeys Him. Then she is ready to touch the forbidden fruit. Finally the temptation seems to be more than she can stand. She reaches out her hand, takes the fruit, and eats it. It tastes delightful. She wonders why she has waited so long. The snake must be right after all. God surely didn't mean to keep her from eating fruit as lovely as this.

She gathers more and offers it to Adam, who also eats it.

No doubt he says, "But I thought God told us not to eat this fruit."

And Eve probably replies, "Oh, it's quite all right. The snake told me I wouldn't die, and, you see, nothing has happened to me. Maybe God made a mistake."

But God had not made a mistake. He had a good reason for telling Adam and Eve not to eat of that tree. It was His way of finding out if they really loved Him. He had given them so much—every good thing He could think of—and He longed for them to love Him in return. Did they really love Him? Would they love Him always? How could He be sure?

Willing obedience is a never-failing test of love. If we really love Father and Mother, we will gladly obey them.

That was why God told Adam and Eve not to eat fruit from that tree. It was a simple test. If they had loved Him sincerely, with all their hearts, they wouldn't have eaten it. Then God would have let them live forever. But because they had disobeyed Him, He knew He could not trust them. They would have to die and go back to the dust from which He had made them. What a sad day that was!

How much was at stake in that little test! If only they had known! But they failed the test. Both of them.

As soon as they eat the fruit, they know something is the matter. Something has gone wrong. For the first time in their lives they feel worried. What will God think of them? they wonder. What will He say to them?

Then comes fear. As the day drags wearily on and evening shadows lengthen, they talk in frightened whispers. Somehow all happiness has suddenly gone out of their lives. For the first time they feel sad, miserable, wretched. Eden holds no joy for them anymore. They want only to run away and hide.

What a pity! Yet isn't this the result of disobedience even today? It just spoils everything, doesn't it?

The Price of Sin

(Genesis 3:8-24)

IT IS beginning to get dark. Already a cool breeze is rustling the leaves. Soon it will be night, and the stars will appear again. But there is no happiness in Eden on this lovely evening. With bowed heads and aching hearts Adam and Eve wander sadly through the forest, where a little while before they had known such perfect joy.

Suddenly they hear a familiar sound. It is God walking "in the garden in the cool of the day."

Until now Adam and Eve have been glad to hear His wonderful voice and have run to meet their much-loved Friend. But now they run away from Him. "They hid from the Lord God among the trees of the garden." It is a foolish thing to do. They cannot hide from God any more than you or I can hide from Him today.

"But the Lord God called to the man, 'Where are you?'"

God does not need to ask. He knows where they are, but He wants them to know that He is looking for them, that He still cares for them and loves them.

What tenderness is in His voice! He seems to be saying, "Why are you hiding from One who loves you so? Why don't you come to meet Me as you used to do?"

Unable to keep silent any longer, Adam steps slowly from his hiding place and says, "I heard you in the garden, and I was afraid."

Afraid! What a strange thing for him to say! He had never been afraid before. He had never known what fear was. Now this grand, noble being, God's masterpiece of Creation, was afraid. And, oh, most sorrowful thought, he was afraid of his Maker!

That is what sin does. It makes people afraid of even their best friends. It turns the bravest person into a coward. It bows the noblest head in shame.

God knows what has happened, of course, for nothing is hidden from Him. But He asks Adam, "Have you eaten from the tree that I commanded you not to eat from?"

Yes, Adam has eaten of the tree. So has Eve. Both have disobeyed God. Sadly they stand before Him, wondering what He will say next, what their penalty will be.

God had warned them, "For when you eat of it you will surely die."* They had often wondered what He had meant by those strange words. Having never seen death, they didn't know what it is like. Are they going to die now? Will today be their last day upon the earth? How sad! They had been there such a little while.

Then God tells them what must happen to them because of their sin. He explains how, from the very moment of their disobedience, they have begun to die, and in their hearts they know it is true. They cannot live forever as He had planned they should. Eternal life is not for them. Not now. Already they are dying, and they will return at last to the dust from which He had made them. It will take a long time, many hundreds of years, but this will be their fate.

Meanwhile they will have to leave their beautiful home. Instead of the pleasant, easy time they have had, they will have to work hard and long for their living. They will know pain and sorrow. They will learn the awfulness of sin as they see all nature suffer with them because of what they have done.

Looking at Adam in deepest pity, God says, "Because you listened to your wife and ate from the tree about which I commanded you, 'You must not eat of it,' cursed is the ground because of you; through painful toil you will eat of it all the days of your life. It will produce thorns and thistles for you, and you will eat the plants of the field. By the sweat of your brow you will eat your food until you return to the ground, since from it you were taken; for dust you are and to dust you will return."

Is God too hard on them? No. He knows the deadly nature of sin, how it wrecks and spoils everything it touches. He had seen it break the sweet harmony of heaven.

Now it is beginning on earth, threatening to ruin this glorious Paradise He has just created. Something has to be done. Adam and Eve must be made to realize what sin means, what it does, and what it costs.

It is all very sad. I don't know who feels worse as the two poor creatures turn from God and begin to walk away from their beautiful Eden home. Darkness is gathering, and from out of the forest peer many animal friends. Their wonder-filled eyes seem to ask each other, What is the matter? Where are they going? Even the birds hush their twittering. They listen in awe to the great, heartbroken sobs of their lord and master as he and his lovely wife walk out into the night.

For Adam and Eve the hardest thing to bear is the thought that they cannot return. By morning Eden will be only a memory. They will never enter it again.

Turning to take one last look at all they have loved and lost, they see a strange light glowing in the darkness along the way they have come. It looks like a fiery weapon held in an angel's hand. It is a flaming sword "flashing back and forth to guard the way to the tree of life."

The way is closed; the gate is locked. How great is the cost of one little sin!

---

* Genesis 2:17.

One Gleam of Hope

(Genesis 3:15, 21)

HOW FAR Adam and Eve wandered from their Eden home we are not told, but they soon noticed many changes. For one thing they found they needed clothes, and we read that "the Lord God made garments of skin for Adam and his wife and clothed them."

What wonderful clothes these must have been, made with all the skill, all the thoughtfulness, all the tender pity of the Creator! Yet these clothes meant death. At least one animal, maybe even two or more, had to die so Adam and Eve could live. Again Adam and Eve saw the terrible cost of sin.

Many times they must have talked about the good old days they had enjoyed in the glorious Paradise God had given them in the beginning. They must have often wondered whether they would ever be allowed to see it once more.

Again and again they went over all that had happened on that sad day when they had made their terrible mistake, and one thing kept coming back to their minds. It was something God had said to the snake. Over and over they repeated it: "I

will put enmity between you and the woman, and between your offspring and hers; he will crush your head, and you will strike his heel."

What could this mean?

One thing was certain. It meant that Eve would have children, and she was glad for that. But how much more did it mean? Well, there would be "enmity," or war, between Eve's children and the snake's children. Eve knew that she would never forgive the snake for the way he had deceived her and robbed her of her lovely home. Her children wouldn't either. She would see to that. And she was confident that when God said to the snake, "He will crush your head," it meant that her seed, her children—or one of them—would win the conflict at last.

Here, for the first time, she saw a gleam of hope. Someday the wicked snake who had brought such sorrow and loss upon her and her husband would be destroyed. Then, perhaps, God would let them go back to Eden.

How they both loved this promise! It was the first promise ever made to mankind and the first one mentioned in the Bible. To Adam and Eve it was the *only* promise they had, and how precious it must have been to them! On dark days, when everything seemed to go wrong, they remembered it and talked about it until hope sprang up in their sorrowing hearts once more.

You can imagine how eagerly they looked forward to having their first baby. Perhaps *he* would be the one—when he grew up—to crush the snake's head. Maybe they wouldn't have

75

Adam and Eve often talked about the promise God made to them just before they were driven out of the Garden of Eden. Eve clearly remembered how God cursed the serpent, and why.

to wait very long to return to Eden after all!

But when Cain was born he did not crush the snake. Instead he turned out to be a big disappointment. Nor did Abel, or Seth, or any of their other children fulfill the promise. The years went by, and still no one came to restore them to Paradise and the tree of life. It must have been hard to keep on hoping.

What was it God had in mind when He made that promise in the Garden? Whom was He talking about when He spoke of the woman's seed? God was thinking of His own Son, and how one day He would come to earth as a baby—one of Eve's children—and Himself fight the great enemy. As Jesus Christ, Immanuel, "God with us," He would destroy Satan and bring Adam and Eve and all who love God back to Eden.

Of course, if God had said to Adam and Eve, "You will have to wait thousands of years before you see your home again," they would have been too discouraged. So He told them just enough to know that all would be well at last. This cheered their poor, sad hearts and led them to keep on hoping.

Men and women have passed on the same blessed hope from one to another down the ages. This is how it came about that all the people who loved God—even those who lived long ago—began looking forward to the coming of Jesus. This is why "Enoch, the seventh from Adam," said, "See, the Lord is coming with thousands upon thousands of his holy ones to judge everyone." [1]

Today we have the same hope. Everywhere boys and girls who love Jesus look eagerly for His return. When He

comes, the promise that God made to Adam will be fulfilled,
and "that ancient serpent called the devil," [2] will be
destroyed. Then Eden—beautiful, glorious Eden—will be
restored, and the children of God will live there in perfect
happiness forever. ✐

[1] Jude 1:14, 15
[2] Revelation 12:9

77

The First Baby

(Genesis 4:1)

WHEN God created the fish, birds, and animals, He said to them, "Be fruitful and increase in number." [1]

Before long thousands of baby fish, tiny minnows, and infant whales were swimming and playing in the rivers and seas. In the trees and bushes of the forest, birds of every kind and color began to build nests. They laid their eggs and hatched them, as birds have done through all the centuries from that day to this.

To the first sheep came the first little lambs, to the first bears came cuddly little cubs, to the first elephants came cute little baby elephants—and so on through all creation. The whole world became one big nursery, with thousands of mothers and fathers doing their best to feed and train their children.

God also told Adam and Eve, "Be fruitful and increase in number." [2] He didn't want them to be alone. Instead He wanted them to have a large family and enjoy the love and companionship of many, many boys and girls.

79

← PAINTING BY RUSSELL HARLAN

The first family was a busy one. Father Adam cultivated the soil, his boys learned how to plant the seeds that grew and provided them food to eat, and Mother Eve kept the home.

When you stop to think of it, this was by far the greatest gift of God's love to these dear creatures He had made. Better than all the beauties of nature, better than all the rich stores of gold and silver, better than all the friendship of the animals, was the ability to have boys and girls who would one day grow up to be men and women like themselves.

God knew that this most precious gift could bring them endless happiness. Their joy would expand with their family, as their children and their children's children grew to love and honor them through all time to come.

We do not know how many children Adam and Eve had, but from what we are told, we may be sure that they had lots and lots of them. And what bright and beautiful children they must have been, offspring of these two majestic beings formed by the Creator Himself! How the hills and valleys rang with their happy laughter as they romped together in the fields and woods and played with their animal friends!

Of all their children we know the names of only three boys. Of course, they must have had girls in their family too, but we can't find any of their names in the Bible. The name of their first baby—the very first ever born on this earth—was Cain. It's no wonder we know *that* name, for first babies are always so very important, aren't they?

How Adam and Eve loved that little boy! How they must have counted his fingers and toes! How they marveled at the beauty of his eyes, his nose, his ears, his mouth, time and time again, just as all fathers and mothers have admired their first babies ever since!

80

THE FIRST BABY

I feel sure that the Son of God took many a tender look at that soft little bundle of loveliness in Eve's arms. He knew that someday He would come to live among the children of Adam and Eve in just the same way.

Little Cain must have been a great comfort to the sad hearts of his parents. The very joy of looking at him, playing with him, and loving him must have helped them forget their sorrows. They thought of the day when he would grow up to be a fine big boy, a young man just like his noble father. What wonderful dreams, what great hopes for the future they must have cherished in their hearts for this firstborn son!

But their dreams never came true. Instead, this dear, dear treasure, this joy of their hearts, gave them their greatest sorrow.

They thought they had paid the price of sin when God had driven them from the Garden of Eden, but they had only begun to pay it. Soon, all too soon, they were to see what sin can do in a child's life, what it can do to a child's home, what it can do to the parents' hearts.

Oh, sad, sad story! This beautiful baby, this perfect child, first-born of the world's first man and woman, became the world's first murderer.

---

[1] Genesis 1:22.
[7] Genesis 1:28.

The First Quarrel

(Genesis 4:2-8)

THE SECOND little boy whose name we find in the Bible was Abel. He was born fairly soon after Cain, because the two grew up together. They must have played in the woods and paddled in the streams together. Perhaps they were the first little boys to make a boat and float it on the nearest pond. What a wonderful time they had in those far-off days when the world was young and so very, very beautiful!

These two boys were probably leaders in Adam and Eve's large and growing family. Younger brothers and sisters looked up to them and followed their example. This may be the reason their names and none of the others are recorded. Because they were leaders, the way they lived and acted became very important.

As time went on and the boys grew to manhood, they turned to different interests. Cain loved to grow things. The Bible says he "worked the soil." Probably he invented the first plow. How thrilled he must have been to gather seeds, sow

83

While Cain and Abel were both offering sacrifices on their altars God sent fire from heaven and accepted Abel's offering. This made Cain jealous and angry with his brother.

them, and watch them grow into strong, sturdy, beautiful plants.

Abel, we are told, liked to work with animals. He "kept flocks," which made him the first shepherd. I imagine he took special care of his baby lambs.

Both boys had been told about God. Most of Eve's bedtime stories were probably about Eden and all that had happened there. Those glorious days in that wonderful garden were her most precious memories.

These two boys, as well as all her other children, learned of the loving Creator. She told them about the devil's temptation, how she yielded to it, and of all the sad things that happened afterward.

Of all Eve's stories, one must have been the children's favorite. It was about God's promise that someday one of her children would crush the snake's head and lead the family back to their Eden home. Every child must have hoped he or she would be that hero.

The children learned to give offerings to God in order to show their love and respect for Him and their faith in His promise to help them. Time and again they were told that sin is so hateful that only death—the shedding of blood—could bring an end to it.

"In the course of time Cain brought some of the fruits of the soil as an offering to the Lord. But Abel brought fat portions from some of the firstborn of his flock. The Lord looked with favor on Abel and his offering, but on Cain and his offering he did not look with favor."

HERBERT RUDEEN

THE FIRST QUARREL

Just how God showed "favor" to Abel's offering the Bible does not say. Maybe fire came down from heaven and consumed it. Anyway, there was a difference. It was clear that Cain's offering of fruits, nuts, and vegetables was not welcome.

Why did God make this difference? Why did He favor one offering and not the other? Abel's sacrifice was part of God's plan to show Adam's family how He would defeat Satan and win Eden back. This sacrifice reminded them that God would provide a way to save Adam's sinful family by giving His own Son, "the Lamb of God,"* to die in their place.

Cain, no doubt, understood this just as clearly as Abel, but he couldn't see why his offering wouldn't work just as well as his brother's. When he saw that God had favor for Abel's offering but ignored his own, he was filled with jealousy.

"So Cain was very angry, and his face was downcast." Cain looked as angry as he felt—which was very angry.

God saw those ugly looks, just like He sees all ugly looks today. He said to Cain, "Why are you angry? Why is your face downcast? If you do what is right, will you not be accepted? But if you do not do what is right, sin is crouching at your door."

God was trying to be fair. He wasn't playing favorites. Cain had the same opportunities as Abel. If he had brought the same offering, God would have accepted it, as He had accepted Abel's.

But Cain was in no mood to be reasoned with. He was so angry he couldn't think clearly. He thought that he was right and God was wrong, and he was sure Abel had played some trick to win God's favor.

Cain went over to where Abel was standing and said, "Let's go out to the field." What else he said we have not been told. But we can be sure it was nothing pleasant or brotherly. His voice rose. He called names. He made false charges. It was the first quarrel.

Cain became more and more angry, until at last he "attacked his brother Abel and killed him." Whether he struck him with his fist or a club, or stabbed him with a knife, the Bible doesn't say. We are left with a picture of that tall, handsome youth sagging limply to the ground.

Death had come to the human family. The first home had been broken for the first time. Oh, sad, sad day!

Who brought the news to Adam and Eve nobody knows, but the shock to them must have been terrible. I can see them running out to that bloodstained field and picking up the poor, stiffening body. They couldn't believe it would never breathe, never smile, never speak to them again.

I can hear the heartbroken sobs of that poor father and mother as they cried, much as King David years later would cry for Absalom, "O my son Abel! My son, my son Abel! If only I had died instead of you—O Abel, my son, my son!"

_____
* John 1:29.

The Marked Man

(Genesis 4:9-16, 25)

CAIN was terrified at what he had done. As he saw his brother's body collapse to the ground, he wondered what had happened. He had never seen a person die before. Then the awful truth dawned upon him that Abel was dead—dead like the lamb on Abel's altar.

Cain's anger turned to fear and remorse. He couldn't go back home. Not now. He could not face his father and mother after doing this dreadful thing. He couldn't face his brothers and sisters, for they would be angry with him. Perhaps they would want to kill him as he had killed Abel. He would have to run away as far as he could go and never come back.

That is what sin does. It separates loved ones, wrecks happiness, drives peace from the mind and joy from the heart.

As Cain fled from the scene he heard God calling to him, "Where is your brother Abel?"

"I don't know," said Cain, as though he could lie to God. Then he said rudely, "Am I my brother's keeper?"

"What have you done?" asked God. "Your brother's blood

cries out to me from the ground."

Of course God knew all the time what had happened. We can hide nothing from Him. He had witnessed Cain's dreadful deed. He had seen Abel's blood on the ground, and it cried out for justice. In the silence and helplessness of death, Abel cried louder than if he had been alive. Something had to be done about this great wrong.

Cain had broken the sixth commandment of God's holy law: "You shall not murder."* But by his pride, his jealousy, his anger, his selfishness, and his lying, he had broken all the other nine as well. He had to be punished. But how?

"Now you are under a curse and driven from the ground," God said. "When you work the ground, it will no longer yield its crops for you. You will be a restless wanderer on the earth."

In His mercy God did not take Cain's life, but sent him away from his home and from all who had been so dear to him. This was just what had happened when Adam and Eve sinned and God sent them away from the Garden of Eden. The lad was

to be a fugitive, forever running for his life—a vagabond, a tramp, who never dared settle down.

"My punishment is more than I can bear," Cain cried as he realized what his sin had cost him. "Today you are driving me from the land, and I will be hidden from your presence; I will be a restless wanderer on the earth, and whoever finds me will kill me."

Poor Cain pictured himself as living in constant fear of losing his life. He would always be running farther and farther from the home to which he could never return.

Out of pity for this youth who had been so dear to Him from babyhood, God "put a mark on Cain so that no one who found him would kill him." Just what this mark was the Bible does not say. Maybe it was a change in his face, which sin, remorse, and worry always bring.

Whatever it was, from this moment on he was a different man, the first marked man in history. Marked, not so he could be caught and punished, but marked by his punishment so he could be spared.

The mark did something else. It reminded Cain, his wife, his children, and all who would ever meet him, how awful sin is. It was a warning never to follow the evil thoughts that had brought so much sorrow upon Cain and his loved ones.

"So Cain went out from the Lord's presence and lived in the land of Nod, east of Eden."

Did you ever stop to think what that meant to Adam and

Eve? In one brief day they lost two sons. Abel was dead. Cain, their firstborn, on whom they had depended so much and on whom they had pinned their hopes for the future, was an outcast. He was running toward the unknown lands in the east for fear of his life.

What a dark day that must have been! Not since that awful night when they had taken their last look at Eden had they felt such loneliness and despair. Perhaps they even wondered whether life was worth living and what the use was of hoping anymore.

But hope came again to their poor, sad hearts—in the form of a baby. Soon Eve had another little boy. The Bible says, "And she gave birth to a son and named him Seth, saying, 'God has granted me another child in place of Abel, since Cain killed him.' "

So they started again, believing and hoping that this might be the baby through whom the promised seed would come. And this time, though they did not know it, they were right. 🌿

---

* Exodus 20:13.

Adam's Last Birthday

(Genesis 5)

WHEN the little boy Seth was born, Adam was 130 years old. That sounds very old to us, but it wasn't old in those days. Adam was just beginning his life. He lived 800 years after that.

It may seem hard to believe, but on Adam's last birthday he was 930 years old. If he had had a birthday cake with candles on it, what a sight it would have been!

Perhaps you are saying, "Nobody could have lived that long!" But wait a minute. Remember, Adam was the first human, created by God Himself on the sixth day of Creation week. He was the most perfectly formed man who ever lived. His heart, his lungs, his muscles, fresh from God's own hands, were made to last forever. They *would* have lasted forever if he had not sinned. Except for that one sad mistake, he could have eaten of the tree of life and lived on and on and on.

Besides, in the beginning of the world's history no one had the diseases we have now that cause so many people to die very young. For hundreds of years Adam probably never knew what it was to be sick. Most likely he never had a cold, or flu, or measles, or chicken pox, or even a toothache.

So wonderfully had God made Adam that he kept his marvelous health and strength for most of his long, long life. Only old age weakened him until he finally died and returned to the dust from which he had been made.

Since Adam lived to be more than 900 years old, he must have seen not only his children grow to adulthood but also his grandchildren, his great-grandchildren, and his great-great-grandchildren. By the time he died he must have been a great-great-great-great-great-grandfather. I really don't know how many "greats" to put in.

If he celebrated his nine hundred thirtieth birthday by inviting all his relatives, thousands upon thousands of people would have attended. You see, since everyone on earth was descended from Adam, they were all related to each other — brothers and sisters, aunts and uncles, nephews and nieces, cousins and half cousins. The population of the earth in that far-off day was made up of one big family, with Adam the grand old father of them all.

Not only did Adam live a long time, but so also did his children. Seth, that little boy who came to cheer his heart after he lost both Cain and Abel, lived to be 912. And one of Seth's sons, Enos, lived to be 905.

Others who lived a long, long time were Cainan, 910 years; Mahalalel, 895; and Jared, 962. The man who lived longest of all was Methuselah, who lived to be 969—almost a thousand years. Then there were Lamech, 777, and Noah, 950.

You can read about these grand old men in the fifth chapter of the book of Genesis. When you do, take a pencil and paper and draw lines to show how long each of them lived. Allow half an inch (or two centimeters) to a hundred years. Work it out carefully, and you will discover some very interesting facts.

First, you will notice that of the nine patriarchs mentioned in this chapter, eight of them lived at the same time as Adam. Only Noah never saw him.

Second, you will see that two of them, Methuselah and Lamech, not only knew Adam personally, but lived almost to the time of the Flood.

Third, you will see that Noah was 600 years old when the Flood came, and he lived 350 years after it.

What does all this mean? It means that everyone in those far-off days must have known about the story of Creation. Everyone must have known about Eden and God's wonderful goodness to Adam and Eve in the glorious garden He made for them. Everyone must have known about their temptation and fall. And, most important of all, everyone must have known about God's promise to win back all that Adam and Eve so carelessly threw away.

From father to son, from one patriarch to another, the wonderful story was handed down. There was never any excuse for sin, never a reason why anyone should not know God and love Him with all his or her heart.

The Man Who
Walked Into Heaven

(Genesis 5:20-26)

I F YOU drew those lines I suggested, you will see that one line is much shorter than all the others—the line marking the life of Enoch. His father lived to be 962, and his son 969, but he lived only 365 years.

Why was this? Did he get ill and die early?

No. In fact, he didn't die at all. That was the wonderful thing about Enoch. The Bible says, "God took him away," which means that he didn't have to die.

That is something to think about. God does not treat everybody like that. As far as we know, only two people in all the history of the world—Enoch and Elijah—never died.

Why did God take Enoch? He must have had a very good reason for treating Enoch differently. Was there something about this man that made God love him more than all the other people of his day?

You may say, "But didn't God love Adam, His masterpiece of Creation, very dearly?" He did. But God let Adam die, just as He said He would, after he had lived 930 years. How about

← PAINTING BY RUSSELL HARLAN

Enoch was a very good man. He loved God and was kind and helpful to his neighbors. He often went into the woods to talk with God in the cool shade and quiet of the trees.

Seth? Wasn't he especially loved too? He was, but God let him die too, after he had lived 912 years. That's what happened with all the others. God loved them, but He let them die.

What was different about Enoch? The Bible doesn't tell us very much about it. It simply says, "When Enoch had lived 65 years, he became the father of Methuselah. And after he became the father of Methuselah, Enoch walked with God 300 years. . . . Enoch walked with God; then he was no more, because God took him away."

There is the secret—he walked with God. That is what God wanted Adam to do from the very beginning. There isn't anything God wouldn't have done for Adam if Adam had walked with Him as Enoch did, instead of forgetting Him and wandering away. Certainly he never would have died.

It was the same way with Seth, Enos, Cainan, and all the rest. God wanted them all to walk with Him, but none of them quite lived up to His expectations.

Only Enoch did. He was different from the others. He loved God with all his heart. He had one purpose: to serve God and do His will. He wanted to be like Him by never being selfish, greedy, jealous, or angry, for he believed that he was a child of God and that such wicked thoughts should not be in his heart.

No wonder God was drawn to this dear man. I can almost hear God saying, "Here is a man after My own heart. He is

96